ONE HUNDRED AND ONE WAYS TO RECYCLE A HOCKEY STICK!

Professor Floydd Mackenzie

Red Deer College Press

The Publishers
Red Deer College Press
56 Avenue & 32 Street Box 5005
Red Deer Alberta Canada T4N 5H5

Acknowledgments
The Publishers gratefully acknowledge the financial contribution of The Alberta Foundation for the Arts, Alberta Culture & Multiculturalism, The Canada Council, Radio 7 CKRD and Red Deer College.

Credits
Designed by Dennis Johnson.
Printed and bound in Canada by Best Gagné Printing Ltée for Red Deer College Press.
Special thanks to Clark Daniels for his assistance in the preparation of this book.

To my Mother, Nellie Mackenzie, without whom none of this would have happened, that's for sure. And to my very special chum, Hilaire.
–Floydd Mackenzie

Canadian Cataloguing in Publication Data
More, David
101 ways to recycle a hockey stick
ISBN 0-88995-089-X
1. Hockey – Humor.   I. Title
GV847.M67 1992   796.962'0207   C92-091325-3

FOREWORD

People grow fond of items that have played significant roles in their lives. This phenomenon has been observed for centuries, worldwide. A certain "affection" sets in toward the inanimate object because of its association with happy or otherwise important events.

We see evidence of this curiosity in the 20th century in the collections of old, derelict automobiles in back-yards throughout North America.

Explanations run something like this: ". . . the '52 Nash, that was my first car, and well, just look at those seats . . . never been anything quite so comfortable . . . and the '49 Desoto, jeez, well just look at her . . . you could hold a dance in the back there, in fact we did . . . and here now, heck, our '62 Volkswagen . . . our son Norm was born in there one windy Tuesday . . . how could we part with any of these? They're family. Besides, they're so USEFUL . . . you never know when you might need a part from one of 'em."

Lost in the vapors of nostalgia is the fact that the last part to be removed was a hubcap (now a geranium pot) back in 1972. The key phrase is: "they're so USEFUL."

Observe how even clothing falls into the same categories of fondness: "That leather jacket . . . there's never been anything like it, and Sheila Dirber carved her initials in the sleeves, and how could you give Sheila away? And this dress . . . remember how Ralph Skirnfeld spilled gin all down the front at the Prom, and I just know the long frills are going to be back in style, so into the closet it goes . . . ."

To their owners, these items have so much potential for returning to their former glory. It's only a matter of time before they're prime candidates for recycling. The logic employed is: "HOW COULD WE, BEING OF SOUND MIND AND BODY, POSSIBLY PART WITH THESE THINGS SIMPLY BECAUSE THEY'VE PASSED BEYOND THEIR INITIAL PURPOSE?"

Astonishing as it may seem to the uneducated, the humble hockey stick falls into this category of "affection/affectation"; that is, the transference of something completely worn out, shot, kaput, dated, obsolete (but through association possessing a "fondness" that gives it human properties) to the realm of alternate usage. Such objects of fondness cry out for recycling.

"That stick in the corner there, with only half a blade left . . . my son Herbert got his first assist in Tiny Mites

with it . . . and over there . . . that stick doing yeoman service behind the furnace . . . remember when Dorothy got the winning goal on that breakaway in the Johnson Feed Mix Tournament . . . . How could you part with that? Especially when its so darn USEFUL!"

Useful. Just how useful are these aging hockey sticks that linger in attics and basements? That's what we here at the International Center for the Correlation of Underused Paraphernalia (ICCUP) wanted to find out. ICCUP obtained the services of Dr. Floydd Mackenzie, a noted Affectologist. Dr. Mackenzie is currently a member of the faculty at the University of East Wink, Saskatchewan, where he teaches Socio-metric Bonding, Welding, and Nuclear Crop Dusting.

Here is his long-awaited report. At last.

ONE HUNDRED AND ONE WAYS TO RECYCLE A HOCKEY STICK

INTERNATIONAL CENTER FOR THE CORRELATION OF UNDERUSED PARAPHERNALIA

ICCUP

A Report by
Dr. Floydd Mackenzie, PH.D., D.AFT.

People's respect (one might almost say reverence) for the hockey stick is quite unique. Much of the affection for the hockey stick seems to stem from its extraordinary structural strength—necessary for its role in a very rough sport—and for the unique proportions and shapes inherent in its design. Unlike many other sports' paraphernalia, the hockey stick in post-sport usage possesses an evolutionary potential similar to the mythical transformation of a weapon into a humble tool . . . somewhat the reverse of the historical Samurai evolution of tools into weapons.

Our research took us to all corners of the globe during the last six years. While the majority of our findings were made on the North American continent, as one would expect, the surprisingly rapid spread of ice hockey to Europe and even to the Asian, African and Australian continents led us to important discoveries worldwide.

We find that the employment of Underused (Unused to full potential, as we prefer to call them) hockey sticks can be categorized in many ways. These categories are based on two factors: the condition of the Unused Hockey Stick (or UHS) after its official life has ended and the social surroundings of the owner(s) of the UHS.

To understand the varying conditions of the UHS we must first familiarize ourselves with its construction. The hockey stick in its pure or "off-the-shelf" form consists of two main parts: the SHAFT and the BLADE.

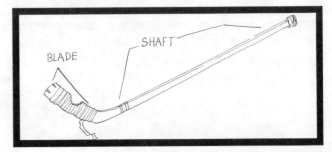

Tape is almost always applied to the hockey stick in its initial stages. The blade is wrapped to enhance its puck-handling qualities, and as the life of the hockey stick progresses (or, more appropriately, regresses), the tape keeps the blade from cracking and splitting.

HOCKEY STICKS—HOW THEY GET THAT WAY. SOMETIMES.

The SHAFT is frequently cut down to lengths appropriate to the player, and then a "knob" of tape is applied at the top end. This knob helps the hockey player hang on to the stick and pick it up from the ice surface with greater alacrity when it is dropped during a game.

When a hockey stick has passed the point of being an effective tool in the game due to breakage or wear, it is then ready to be reexamined and modified for many possible roles as a UHS.

If the stick is broken at a point between the blade and shaft, the general rule of thumb is that quick sawing of both broken ends produces two marvelous sections of UHS. The individual and combined uses are astonishing.

Should the stick remain relatively intact but be worn from excessive use, the whole UHS can be employed in numerous ways.

Some of the functions in which the UHS has been observed include:

1. PROPPING,
2. WEDGING,
3. FLICKING,
4. SCOOPING,
5. PROJECTING,

6. GUIDING and
7. CONGLOMERATIVE RECYCLING (in various combinations)

These activities are best examined under major headings:

1. HOUSEHOLD USAGE—OUTDOOR
2. HOUSEHOLD USAGE—INDOOR
3. HOUSEHOLD USAGE—CONGLOMERATIVE RECYCLING AS FURNITURE
4. GENERAL USAGE—MEDICAL
5. OUTDOOR RECREATION (OTHER THAN HOCKEY)
6. AUTOMOTIVE
7. EXOTIC USES
   A. DOMESTIC
   B. INTERNATIONAL

Each category will be examined under a separate chapter. We note with satisfaction that a single stick may be recycled into many useful products throughout its life, as we'll see when we examine the life story of an average hockey stick.

CONTENTS

Chapter One

STICKING OUT
(Outdoor Uses Around the House)

Surveys of selected North American urban neighborhoods have produced remarkable figures relative to the employment of Unused Hockey Sticks. The average street containing 30 homes was found to have 16.3 Unused Hockey Sticks (UHS) in varying degrees of condition, occupied in a multitude of outdoor operations.

Uses ranged from general maintenance activities around the yard, both summer and winter, to specific functions depending on the length and condition of the surviving part of the UHS.

Following are some of our major outdoor findings.

REPLACEMENT RUNGS FOR LADDER

RUNGS FOR ROPE LADDERS

LITTER PICKER

EAVESTROUGH CLEANER

**FLICKING DOGGY-DOO INTO NEIGHBOR'S YARD
(FROM WHENCE IT CAME)**

STIRRING LARGE POTS OF CHILI SURPRISE FOR THE CHURCH PICNIC
(The reader is reminded to clearly label those sticks to be used for cooking and those to be used for flicking doggy-doo.)

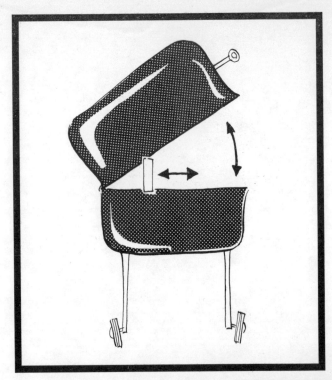

HEIGHT ADJUSTMENT FOR BARBECUE LID
(STUBBY VERSION)

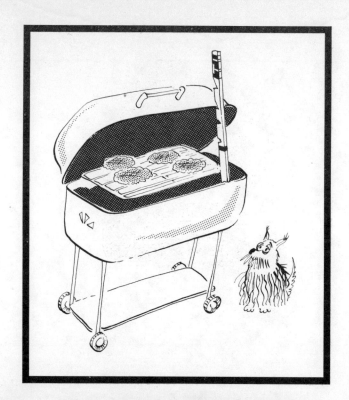

**HEIGHT ADJUSTMENT FOR BARBECUE LID
(NOTCHED VERSION)**

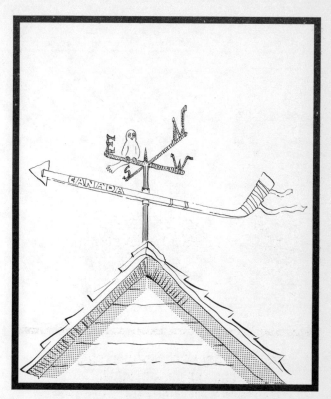

WEATHER VANE

**FRUIT HARVESTER AND FRUIT TREE PROPS
(FOUND IN THE ANNAPOLIS AND OKANAGAN VALLEYS)**

GARDEN HOE AND SCARECROW

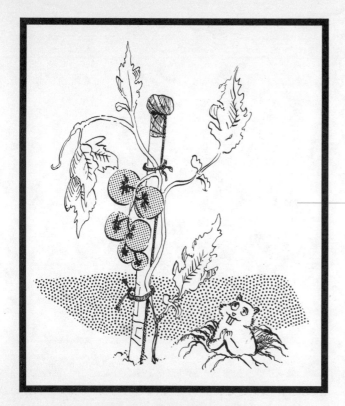

TOMATO PLANT SUPPORT

MAILBOX SUPPORT AND FLAG

YOKE (TWO HOCKEY STICKS SPLICED TOGETHER)

CONCRETE SMOOTHERS (VARIOUS CURVED BLADES MAY BE EMPLOYED FOR SHAPING)

SNOW SHOVEL FOR LIGHT SNOWFALLS

**DRIVEWAY MARKERS—LANDING LIGHTS OPTIONAL
(FOUND IN BRANDON, MANITOBA)**

WINDOW SCRAPER

Chapter Two

STICKING IN
(Indoor Uses Around the House)

Indoor usage of UHS was much more difficult to determine. Observing the use of UHS outdoors, where surveyors could watch unobtrusively, was one thing, but actually persuading people to let researchers into their homes proved to be quite another. Householders were extremely suspicious of our efforts to document uses of the UHS within the home.

But where our surveyors met with success, they conducted thorough basement-to-attic searches and were able to arrive at generalized figures for the application of the UHS indoors.

BACK SCRATCHER

SHOE HORN (CURVED BLADE IS BEST)

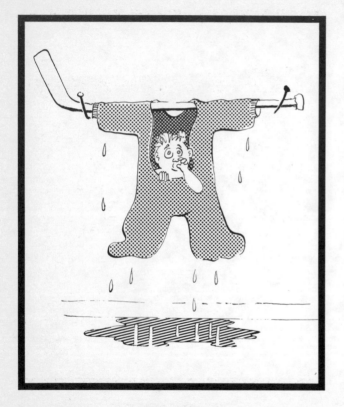

COAT RACK

KID RACK

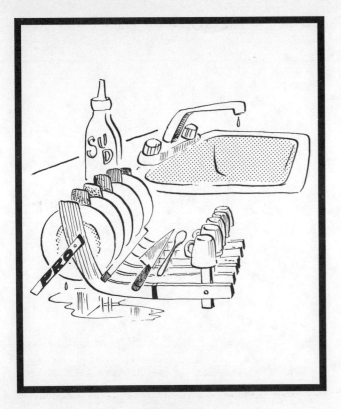

DISH RACK

HOT PIZZA FLIPPER

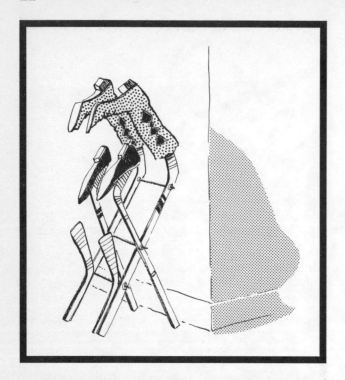

SHOE AND BOOT RACK MADE WITH REINFORCED SPACING ROD (FOUND AT BLUE CORNERS, NORTH DAKOTA)

WINDOW PROPS (NOTE VARIABLE LENGTHS FOR ADJUSTING WINDOW HEIGHT)

OVEN DOOR PROP

TEMPORARY FRIDGE LATCH REPAIR

CALIPERS FOR HOT POTS (BOLTED AT SWIVEL)

LIFTER FOR HOT LIDS (NOTCHED STICK)

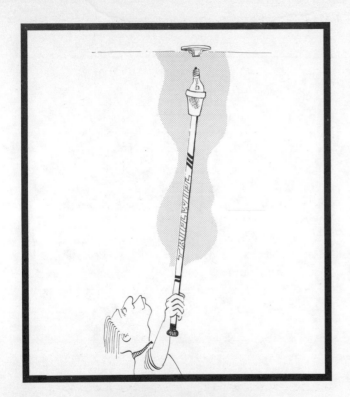

**LIGHT BULB CHANGER WITH
STYROFOAM CUP GLUED TO HANDLE**

DUST PAN (GOALIE STICK WORKS BEST)

DOOR JAMB LOCK FOR SLIDING DOORS

Chapter Three

SITTING PRETTY
(Recycling as Furniture)

On a great many occasions the research team came across examples of "conglomerate recycling" of UHS. This procedure involves inventive combining of old hockey sticks into new structures or devices, particularly in the creation of pieces of furniture. Because of the tensile strength of the hockey stick, it is ideally suited to the creation of furniture items.

These recycled hockey stick furniture items were observed during random household surveys, and additionally some ideas were sent to ICCUP headquarters in response to advertisements placed nationwide by Dr. Mackenzie.

**CHAIR MADE FROM HOCKEY STICKS
(FOUND IN FOGGER'S BLUFF, MICHIGAN)**

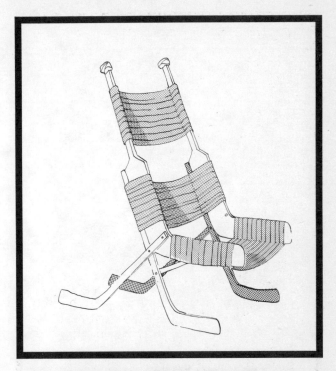

**EASY CHAIR MADE FROM TWO GOAL
STICKS AND FOUR REGULAR STICKS
(FOUND IN STÜNDESKANBÉ, SWEDEN)**

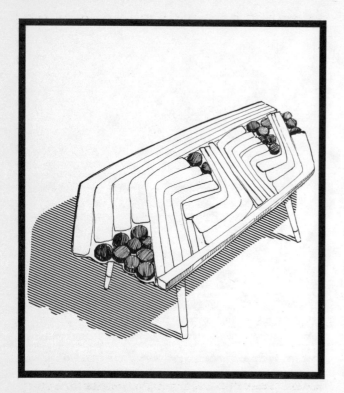

COFFEE TABLE MADE FROM 19 HOCKEY STICKS AND 18.75 PUCKS (FOUND IN NEW BEDSTEAD, ONTARIO)

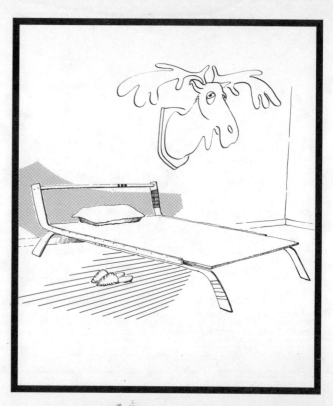

BED MADE WITH SIX STICKS AND PLYWOOD

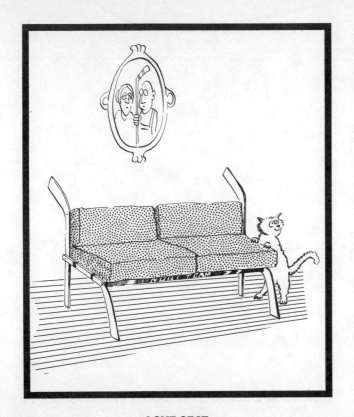

LOVE SEAT

PICTURE FRAMES

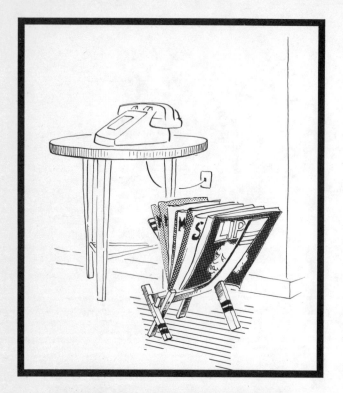

**MAGAZINE RACK MADE FROM TWO STICKS
(FOUND IN DILLY'S COVE, FLORIDA)**

LOG RACK

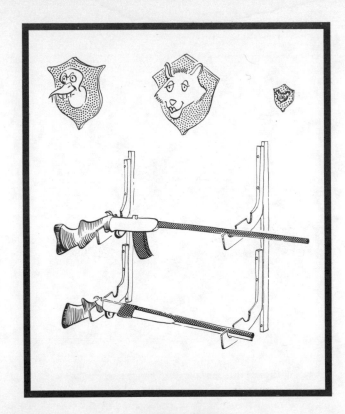

RIFLE RACK

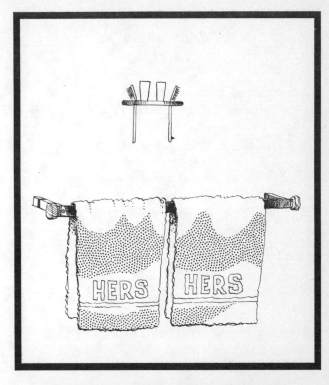

TOWEL RACK (FOUND IN GIRL'S DORMITORY AT TINGLERUDE, OKLAHOMA)

Chapter Four

SLINGS AND ERRORS

(Medical Uses)

The size, shape and strength, plus the availability of hockey sticks, have allowed for their use in a number of medical applications, particularly in the field of Emergency Medicine, in which time and convenience are of the essence.

Many injuries occur at sporting events, on the field or on the ice, or in the stands or bleachers. Whatever the sport, summer or winter, one can bet that someone just happens to have a hockey stick handy.

**EMERGENCY STRETCHER MADE
WITH TWO PAIRS OF PANTS**

SPLENDID SPLINTS

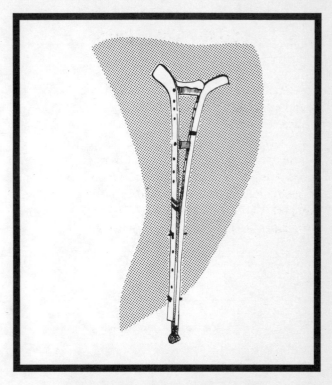

**EMERGENCY CRUTCH MADE FROM
TWO STICKS BOLTED TOGETHER**

**POSTURE RECTIFYING DEVICE
(TO BE WORN WITH TIGHT SWEATER)**

WALKING STICK (CUT TO REQUIRED LENGTH)

CHILDREN'S GROWTH CHART

REFLEX TESTER

**PARABOLIC AID TO HEARING
(CURVED BLADE IS BEST)**

TEMPORARY EYEGLASS REPLACEMENT ARMS
(Prolonged use may cause ears to stick out permanently. This side-effect, however, may actually improve hearing—see Parabolic Aid to Hearing)

VETERINARIAN'S TONGUE DEPRESSOR

Chapter Five

WILD WORLD OF SORTS

(Outdoor Recreation—Other Than Hockey)

Having been designed for portability, the hockey stick's light weight and strength has led to many subsequent support roles in other areas of outdoor recreational activity. Random surveys of campgrounds and playgrounds revealed an average of 2.6 UHS per 50 persons in the summer, and 4.3 UHS per 50 persons in the winter. These figures, of course, did not include any hockey activities, street-wise or rink-wise.

SNOWMAN'S ARMS

**SLED RUNNERS MADE FROM HOCKEY STICKS
(FOUND IN IGPOOLOT, NORTHWEST TERRITORIES)**

TRIPOD FOR OUTDOOR COOKING

TENT POLES

LEAN-TO

FISHING ROD

SAILBOAT TILLER

KAYAK PADDLE

BICYCLE RACK FOR AUTOMOBILE

ROWBOAT OARS

PASSING DRINKS IN A SWIMMING POOL

**SWING SEAT (FROM GOAL STICK) AND
SWING SUPPORT (FROM STICK SHAFT)**

SUPPORTS FOR DUCK BLIND

GOLF BALL RETRIEVER

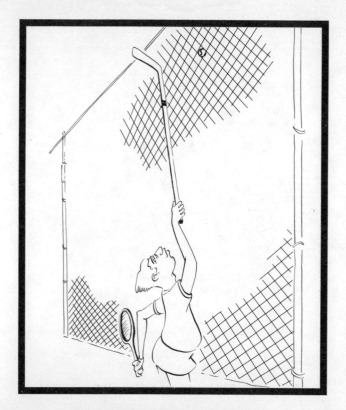

DISLODGING STUCK TENNIS BALLS

EMERGENCY REPLACEMENTS FOR ARCHERY

Chapter Six

WHEELS OF FORTUNE
(Automotive Uses)

Automotive uses for the UHS seem unlimited. Our surveyors constantly unveiled clever applications of hockey sticks in vehicular roles. Some vehicles were seen to employ as many as six UHS at a time. Inventive automobile owners frequently used a single hockey stick for a number of operations in sequence, thereby providing significant examples of harmonic automotive choreography. A sight to behold, indeed.

Our findings have so impressed automobile manufacturers that several are investigating the possibility of including the hockey stick as standard equipment on many models.

To date, some enterprising sales personnel have begun offering a free stick with each new vehicle sold.

Here are but a few of our findings.

HOOD PROP FOR AUTOMOBILES

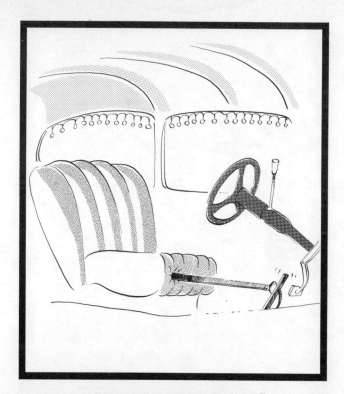

ACCELERATOR JAM FOR COLD WEATHER WARM-UPS

UNLATCHING OPPOSITE DOOR LOCK WITHOUT HAVING TO RELEASE OWN SEAT BELT (EYELET SCREW IN END OF STICK)

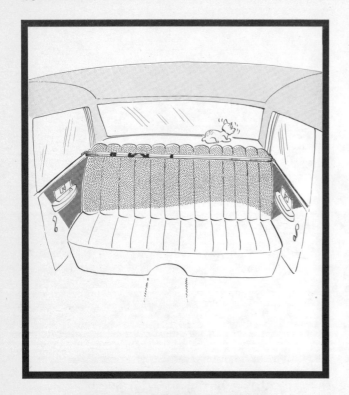

**DOOR LOCKS (HOOKS ON EITHER
END SLIP INTO WINDOW SLOTS)**

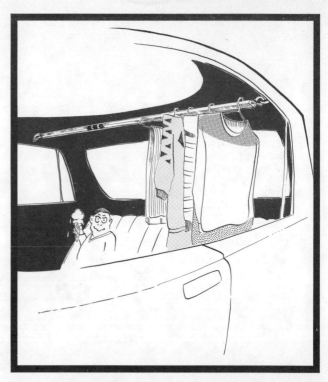

**CLOTHING RACK FOR BACK SEAT
(LARGE EYELET HOOKS ON EITHER END OF STICK)**

**SUN VISOR REPLACEMENT
(GOAL STICK BLADE IS BEST)**

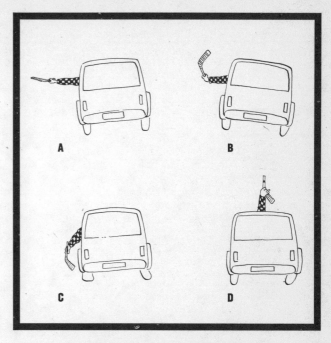

**TURN INDICATOR (REFLECTIVE TAPE
ON STICK BLADE IS A NICE TOUCH)**
(A. Left B. Right C. Stopping D. Your Mother
taught you to drive like the fuzz on a don-
key's earmuff)

HUBCAP REMOVER

BUMPER JACK HANDLE

MANUAL GASOLINE GAUGE FOR A '53 LA FONZA

MEASURING COOLANT IN A '53 LA FONZA

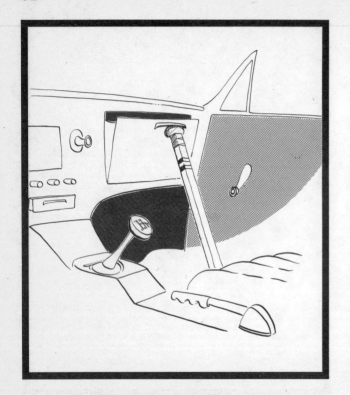

**HOLDING GLOVE COMPARTMENT SHUT
IN A '72 SPUMONI GT**

**HOLDING GEARSHIFT IN 4TH IN A '72 SPUMONI GT
(NOTE NOTCHING AT END OF STICK)**

**HAND BRAKE LEVER REPLACEMENT
IN A '72 SPUMONI GT**

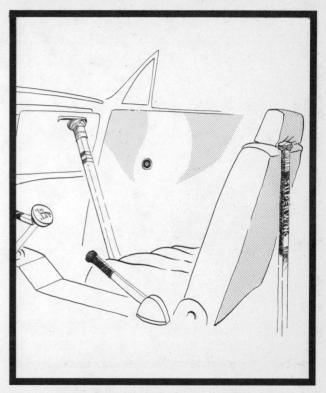

PROP FOR PASSENGER SEAT IN A '72 SPUMONI GT

CURB FEELERS

Chapter Seven

TALES OF THE UNEXPLAINED
(Exotic Uses)

Perhaps the most compelling finds of all took place in unexpected quarters. In many cases a UHS had not only filled in as a stopgap measure for a particular item or project but had in the end supplanted the original part and BECOME the preferred part. We will examine a number of these revelations in this chapter.

Another surprising discovery was the number of occasions in which the hockey stick has shown up in faraway places, often locales that never see ice, never mind hockey players. Research has shown that many times the UHS was transported to the foreign location by a Canadian or American traveling in the area. The traveler, in many cases, having realized the potential usefulness of the hockey stick, simply took it along on the journey. The native population, upon exposure to the hockey stick, was often anxious to barter favorably for it.

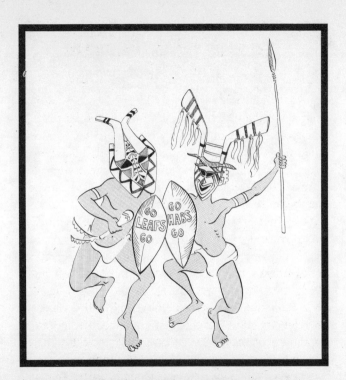

SCARY TRIBAL MASKS MADE FROM HOCKEY STICK BLADES (FOUND IN LOWER JAMJAR PROVINCE, NEW GUINEA)

AUSTRALIAN ABORIGINE THROWING BOOMERANG MADE FROM TWO HOCKEY STICK BLADES
(Note clever splicing of two stick blades found in a boomerang at Keristalmiteymate, Queensland)

**HOCKEY STICK STILT WARRIORS OF
OOOLAN DOODOO, NEW GUINEA**

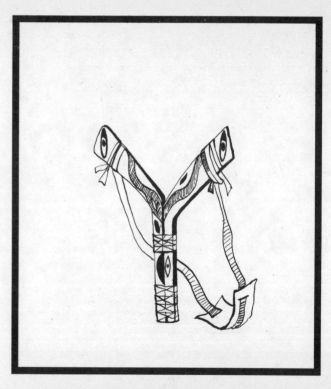

**SLINGSHOT MADE FROM TWO HOCKEY STICKS
(ORIGIN UNKNOWN)**

**CANOE MADE FROM FOUR HOCKEY STICKS
(FOUND IN EAST WACKO ISLANDS)**

**PALANQUIN MADE FROM FOUR HOCKEY STICKS
(FOUND IN LUMPALORE, INDIA)**

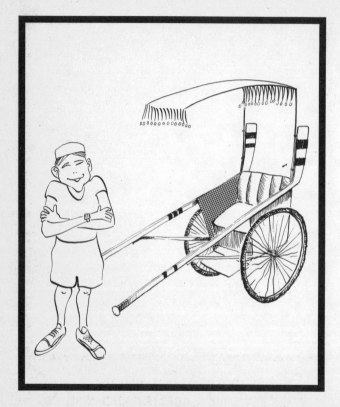

RICKSHAW

INFANT STROLLER

WATER DIVINING ROD MADE FROM TWO HOCKEY STICKS (FOUND IN SHUCKS, WISCONSIN)

CEILING FAN BLADES REPLACED BY HOCKEY STICK BLADES (FOUND IN NUGEY'S BAR AND GRILL, SOUTHROT, MAINE)

SCULPTING TOOLS

HORSIE COMB

PROPELLER BLADES FOR ULTRALIGHT AIRCRAFT

WIRE LIFTER FOR TALL ITEMS

Chapter Eight

BREAKAWAY

(A Life History of a Hockey Stick)

Proving the case for the versatility of the hockey stick, we take you on a well-documented 72-year life history of one particular hockey stick. We shall follow the travails and triumphs of an ingenious amalgam of wood, glue, tape and sweat, and its important roles during threescore and twelve years in the history of the world.

1928 January 14, Waterblot, Manitoba. A shipment of ShurShot hockey sticks from the factory at Poufleneige, Quebec, arrives at Nickersons General Store. Billy Waffle, having saved his $1.28, carefully selects a beautifully crafted, fine-grained ash stick. It is stamped with the endorsement of Wingy Laforge, star forward of the Boston Bruins. The stick has the sweet smell of freshly planed wood. It shoots left.

Billy has five pennies for a roll of hockey tape. He happily bundles his treasures home and there, with care and deliberation, wraps the blade with the sticky black cloth strips.

Billy plans to cut some length from the shaft of the stick. Standing in his skates, he holds the stick upright before him and determines that it should be lopped off at chin height. But wait, he'll grow this year, he's sure, so maybe nose height . . . but this stick will last longer, and in two years he'll be soooo tall . . . . Billy wraps a knob of tape at the top end and leaves the stick full length.

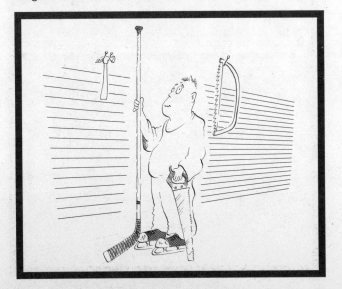

This stick is gonna last forever, Wingy Laforge. Billy decides to name his stick "Wingy," after his hero.

On the frozen ponds around Waterblot, the duo of Billy and Wingy become a daily sight. Billy is too short for Wingy and Wingy is too long for Billy. But on January 23, 1928, Wingy and Billy score their first goal. Both are elated.

1936 NOVEMBER 23, DRUCKER'S POND, MANITOBA. Almost eight years later, Wingy receives a severe crack in his blade. Billy is grief stricken, but Uncle Charlie, the carpenter, repairs Wingy with fish glue and extensive taping. All is well.

1938 Billy discovers girls and takes up the trombone to try to impress them. Billy spends less and less time playing hockey. Wingy is relegated to the basement where he is called on occasionally to prop open the cellar doors.

1941 Billy's popularity with the opposite sex doesn't improve with trombone practice, so he enlists in the Canadian Army, thinking this might impress the ladies. It doesn't. Billy is posted to Nova Scotia for training. He takes his hockey gear along, knowing that sports are a part of army life. Wingy is delighted.

1942 Billy's antiaircraft group is sent to England. Being good Canadians, Billy and his chums take their hockey gear overseas just in case Europe has some ice.

1943 Wingy spends his days tucked under Billy's bunk. He's happy to be near his bosom buddy even if life is dull. There are occasional pickup games with a tennis ball on the parade square, but the cinders are painful to Wingy. He'd rather not.

Wingy is insulted when someone ties a brassiere to him and waves him out the window of a speeding jeep.

Wingy is mortified at being wrapped in cloth and used to clean a Bofors gun barrel. Billy says it's for King and Country, so Wingy feels a little better, but not much.

1944 Billy's group is in Holland among the cheering Dutch people. The Canadians don skates when winter comes and put on several exhibition hockey games along the frozen canals. The Dutch are intrigued. Especially the girls. Billy is pleased. Wingy is delighted. It's just like the good old days. Crisp mornings on smooth ice, slaps of pucks and shouts of happiness.

Billy and a girl named Tina fall in love. They are married in Oosgotajob, and Wingy is decorated with tulips and festooned with ribbons. He and several other hockey sticks form an honor arch of mock lances for the newlyweds. Wingy is delirious with joy.

1945 The war ends. Billy, Wingy and Tina, their new bride, return triumphant to Waterblot.

1948 Billy hasn't played hockey since returning to Canada. Wingy and the trombone sulk in the basement of the Waffle home. Wingy props open the cellar doors on occasion, but the trombone has sat unlipped since 1941. These are tough times.

1950 Billy and Tina become the proud parents of twins, Inga and Hector. Billy, Tina and their new family move to a new house two blocks away. Wingy is used in spare moments, in which he has nothing to do but stir buckets of dirty diapers. He is disgusted. In the summer, there are breezy afternoons when he is taken outdoors to beat rugs. Things could be worse.

1952 The Waffle twins are very mobile now and exploring every part of the house. Inga discovers the trombone and is delighted by its shiny surface under all the layers of dust. She drags it upstairs to put doll's clothing on it. Wingy is alone.

1953 A bad spring flood damages the basement. Wingy is left with a permanent watermark from the grungy water and develops a slight twist and warp in his shaft from being submerged for over a week.

1956 Hector Waffle learns to skate and wants to play hockey. Wingy is astonished to see daylight again. On a bright Sunday afternoon, he is brought out blinking and warped. Billy Waffle carefully removes the old layers of tape from his buddy and applies fresh, new wrappings.

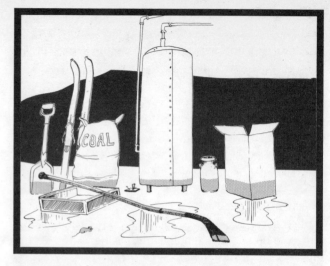

Wingy is presented to Hector in a moment of ceremony. Wingy can't believe his good fortune: the circle is complete. "To you from failing hands we throw . . . ."

1956 THE SAME SUNDAY AFTERNOON. Hector is not fond of Wingy. Unappreciative of Wingy's history and excessive length, and keen to get a new stick just like Jimmy Jenkins has, Hector smacks Wingy against the rink boards and goal posts, and hurls him at building walls. Battered and bruised, Wingy is left out in the snow with Monty, the unappreciated dog. Snow soon covers Wingy, and he disappears for the season. Hector claims Wingy broke and gets a new stick. Billy Waffle gets a faraway look in his eye and makes a ham sandwich.

1957 Spring thaw unveils Wingy. Billy Waffle is excited to find his long-lost friend. Wingy is tossed into a pile of other good stuff in a corner of the garage.

1957 Wingy is revived briefly in the fall, when he is relegated to several weeks of road hockey with Hector and his neighborhood chums. One fateful evening as the sun spreads its glowing arms across the prairie sky, Wingy is jammed against the curb, blade first, and Fat Bennie Gilbert steps on him. There is a loud "Crack!" and then . . . silence. Bennie giggles. Hector curses just like his dad does and tosses the broken stick onto the Waffle lawn.

Mortally wounded, Wingy lies all night, his shaft broken from the blade, where the curve begins. Held by a few splinters and tattered strands of tape, there seems little left to wish for. Perhaps a quick toss onto the burn heap tomorrow when Billy mows the lawn.

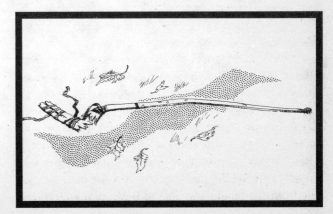

The next day, as he pushes his machine across the final grasses of autumn, Billy comes upon Wingy. He reaches down and tenderly grasps the broken warrior to his chest. He turns Wingy slowly, the shattered blade dangling loosely. "Ah, Wingy . . . what flights of fancy we've had." Unable to throw Wingy away, Billy props him in the dusty corner of the garage, blade and all.

1961 Wingy emerges from a pile of scrap during spring cleaning. In a moment of rare wisdom, Billy suddenly grasps a saw and lops off Wingy's dangling blade.

"Wingy, me lad, I need you to hold open this garage door. The spring is gone." Wingy is revived. Bladeless, warped and stained, but revived. An amputee, yes, but a new purpose, a new beginning.

1964 In a severe windstorm, the garage door snaps down on Wingy, fracturing his shaft nearly in two. He has been halved. It had seemed too good to be true. Back into the corner. Both of him.

1965 All is not lost. With two sharpened ends, Wingy I and Wingy II receive a new lease on life as tomato stakes. It's dirty work sure, but healthy and productive.

After eleven glorious, sun-filled years of garden work, Wingy II is dragged off by a playful Great Dane and never seen again. Wingy I, now just 26 inches long (66 cm) with an old tape knob for a head, continues his declining years supporting tomatoes. Wingy II's replacement is a boring chunk of spruce 1 x 2 named Sid.

1984 Wingy I is accidentally rototilled in the fall. He loses 8 inches (20.3 cm) from his bottom and is now very blunt and splintered.

1985 At eighteen inches (45.7 cm) and a knob, Wingy "What's Left" is resawn and put to work propping open a garage window on hot days. He spends most of his time lying on a window ledge.

1986 Billy Waffle retires from his life-long job at the Noodle Works.

1991 New windows are put in the garage. Wingy is no longer needed but continues to lie on the ledge, joined by a screwdriver named Phil and a pair of needlenose pliers called Delores.

1992 Billy and Tina buy a 52-foot motor home to travel to Arizona in the winters. While packing up Phil and Delores to put into the toolbox, Wingy is accidentally grabbed and tossed in too.

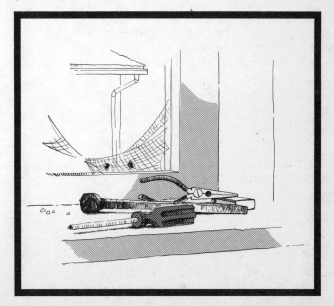

1993 Wingy comes in very handy when he is used to pound a hubcap back onto the motor home. His head hurts. Kept out of the toolbox now, he joins Billy and Tina on the patio of their Arizona mobile home, where he braces a broken deck chair. He enjoys the sunshine there, but he's not ready to retire. Not yet.

1994 Tina buys a new deck chair. Wingy moves over to barbecue duty, propping open the lid.

1995 Tina runs off with the number-caller from the Sun Hills Bingo Palace. A fat guy named Raoul.

1996 Billy marries Lodia Souffle, a widow from Squint, Wyoming.

1999 In spite of the years of intermittent heat, Wingy enjoys the proximity to Billy and Lodia (and their poodle, Snuffy) and the good cheer he brings in providing charbroiled food to his retired chums.

2000 An earthquake measuring 5.3 on the Richter Scale shakes the mobile home park. Wingy falls into the barbecue coals and burns up. Ash to ashes.

As he eats his hamburger, Billy Waffle gets a faraway look in his eye and calculates that in two months the ice will be on the ponds in Waterblot, Manitoba.

The pen behind Professor Floydd Mackenzie belongs to David More, an artist and humorist living in Red Deer, Alberta. He brings to the art of recycling hockey sticks his experience as illustrator and coauthor of five previous books with Eric Nicol, including the best-selling *The Joy of Hockey* and *Golf – The Agony and the Ecstasy*. Over the last twenty years he has seen his artwork join major institutional and corporate collections, as well as The Canada Council's Canada Art Bank. He has been an instructor at the Alberta College of Art and at Red Deer College. An exhibition of his paintings is currently touring museums across Canada.